DYING

TO

LIVE

Is the end of our life on Earth the beginning of another life somewhere else that never ends?

—James Downey

DYING TO LIVE
By James Downey
Copyright ©2022

ISBN: 978-1-950105-27-4
Line Editing Pat Fogarty
Cover Design Pat Fogarty
Granite Publishing
Prescott & Dover
9 8 7 6 5 4 3 2 1
HB1551065906

Acknowledgments

My sincere appreciation to all who contributed their help and support for Dying to Live. Thanks to my dear wife, Pat, author Bruce Paul, and good friends Chuck Seeger and Jack Russell for their encouragement, insightful observations, and input. Thanks also to David Duryee for his editing and wordsmithing skills. Special thanks to Patrick Fogarty for his help in the final configuration, cover design, and for his tireless leadership of the Central Arizona Writers.

Contents

Preface

The phone call came as I was preparing for our neighborhood Independence Day block party. A widower in seemingly good health who lived across the street had unexpectedly passed away. Several neighbors gathered in front of his house, attracted by the flashing lights of the emergency vehicles that responded to the 9-1-1 call from his son.

Our conversation was rather uncomfortable, drifting into cliches—*"It was good he didn't suffer a long illness"*... *"He was so lonely since his wife passed away."* We sidestepped the *"elephant in the room"*— what's next after our demise. From the unspoken cliché— "He's in a better place now"—several implications emerge: (1) there indeed exists a better place; (2) the speaker intimately knows the decedent's heart; (3) both know the path to that better place; and, (4) they know the truth. Absent these four elements, such cliche is simply palliative rhetoric.

The subject of death tends to generate spontaneous barriers that mitigate its discussion or even its contemplation. We each have, it seems, a built-in avoidance mechanism that allows us to live our entire lives in continual denial that we have an expiration date that draws closer every day. Yet there is no guarantee we will see tomorrow. Every day, life-ending events strike young and old, rich and poor, ordinary and famous people, without warning. But not us, right? We fool ourselves that we are somehow exempt from an untimely death, and will have plenty of time to ponder our future demise. After all, the odds favor us reaching our expected life spans—77 years for males, 82 years for females. Our age certainly affects our inclination to think about life's end. During the Vietnam War, males 18 to 26 years old were drafted into military service. That demographic group is targeted primarily because young adults tend to foolishly assume they're invincible. But none of us are.

If you are in that age group, or even in your 30s or 40s, chances are you know someone close to your age who died unexpectedly before *"their time."* Myriad circumstances, including the onset of war, becoming a homicide victim, or succumbing to the coronavirus pandemic can make our age-irrelevant. Many people have developed an almost paralyzing fear of dying from the pandemic.

But is there more to the question? Would you like to have an advantage on living in a broken world that is crumbling before our eyes? What if there is one critical choice during our lives that can not only erase the fear of dying, but can also guide us through life with purpose, hope, and confidence as we navigate life's challenges. More importantly, what if your time to make that choice is approaching expiration? Many believe evidence exists to support this. If even part of this is true, why are we so eager to avoid the profound questions of our existence?

I began asking these same questions when I was a teenager. As I progressed through college, I was drawn into the notion that my secular philosophy and psychology textbooks, and professors had the answers. Scraping by as a student surrounded by worldly examples of financial success led me to *"chase the dream."* I wanted what *"those people"* had, and more.

My chase was derailed from time to time by life's upheavals such as being drafted into the Army during the Vietnam War and episodes of unemployment, accompanied by the anxious churning of, *"how do we get through this?"* All the while, the world kept telling me that if I just had more—more money, a newer car, a Harley, a prestigious house, travel to exotic destinations, that contentment was guaranteed. But it never turned out that way. There was always something missing, overshadowed by a persistent edgy uncertainty when things got shaky or money got tight.

After years of pursuing the wrong things, I returned to my search for meaning. The answers I had been convinced were right had turned out to be misguided and hopelessly shallow. I analyzed, compared, and distilled diverse spiritual books, doctrines, sermons, and viewpoints.

What I found completely changed my life and gave me a new focus and purpose, as well as peace, comfort, and contentment. Neither the present world chaos, today's troubles or those on the horizon, nor the certainty of death hold the same tension they once did.

In addition to my newfound freedom, I have witnessed profound life changes in others brought about by the same factors. Broken lives devastated by drug and alcohol addiction set free of bondage; miraculous recoveries from (according to the attending doctors) fatal drug overdoses with no hope of survival; suicidal thoughts averted by learning that everyone's life has a purpose and a value that is not defined by repeated failures or what others may think or say. Such is the power of what I and others have found. Hopefully, this book will help you to do the same.

Despite the many beliefs about what lies beyond our life on Earth, there is but one ultimate, unavoidable truth as to what awaits us. That truth exists regardless of our beliefs.

Unraveling it will require patience and persistence as you revisit human history spanning thousands of years. Your reward will come if this journey leads you to discover how you fit into the cosmos and your path to a secure life without fear of death. *"The truth will set you free."*

Our Beliefs Are Limited Only By Our Imagination

Individuals, as well as entire cultures, develop divergent views of where people go after they die. They may range from thinking that the lights just go out and that's it, to a belief that people are recycled or reincarnated into another person or creature, depending on how *"good"* or *"bad"* their previous life. I encountered a striking example of one cultural view during a recent visit to the Middle East.

Thousands of years ago, the Egyptian empire gifted the world with monumental architectural and artistic wonders unparalleled to this day. The pyramids, the pharaohs' tombs, the palaces, the Sphinx, and the artifacts in the Cairo Museum must be viewed in person to appreciate their magnificence. Central to all of them is that ancient culture's preoccupation with polytheism, the journey into the afterlife, and the preparations they believed were required for that journey.

Construction of the tombs of Egyptian royalty, which are art museums in their own right, commenced when the royal dignitaries took office and continued to the time of their death. Their flamboyant multi-layered coffins and cavern-like tombs were decorated with intricate paintings and carvings of their most important gods. Even today, that artwork retains much of its original vibrant color and gold-leaf overlays. The royal tombs were filled with furniture, jewelry, and other items assumed to be of value in their next phase of existence.

In contrast to the ancient Egyptians' fixation upon that journey stands our Western inclination to eschew the subject. We have so many earthly pursuits far more pleasurable to contemplate until that time arrives when we are forced by imminent death to confront it.

The answers that we eventually accept as to what lies beyond the grave depend upon our response to questions fundamental to our world view, i.e.:

• Does God truly exist? If so, what is He like?

• Is there one religious text that truly contains God's word among the many which make that claim?

• What is the Bible? Can it be trusted?

• Don't science and evolution explain everything?

• What's all this talk about the "end times?"

This tutorial summarizes insights, analyses, and conclusions regarding these questions by people far more knowledgeable than myself. They are grounded in logic and supported by evidence—my traditional frame of reference as a retired attorney. If you are skeptical about any of it, so was I at one time. There's nothing to lose by keeping an open mind. My intent is not to convince you of anything. It is simply an invitation to consider what is being offered. You must determine what to do with the information.

Does God Exist?

Blaise Pascal, (1623-1662), a 17th-century French philosopher, theologian, mathematician, and physicist, presented a philosophical argument known as Pascal's Wager, positing that people wager with their lives that God either exists or He does not. At stake is one's eternal destiny in heaven or hell. Pascal offers an extended analysis of mankind's unavoidable mandate to decide and the consequences and dynamics of each choice, but he never solidly settles the issue. Almost 400 years later, the debate continues. The consequences remain profound.

If we believe that God does not exist, mathematically there is a 50% chance we are wrong. He either exists, or He does not. The challenge comes from weighing the evidence. The clash between God's word—the Bible—and the secular theory of evolution, is at the crux of the question. The first words of the Bible, in the book of Genesis, state: *"In the beginning, God created the heavens and the earth."* Genesis goes on to describe God's creation of all plants, animals, and the first two human beings, Adam and Eve. This is contrary to secular dogma that the universe and life on earth emerged from random, chance events.

The popular notion that the universe came into existence by a chance event, known as the *"Big Bang Theory,"* is based on the premise that all matter in the universe was once concentrated into one super-dense infinitely small core of mass that exploded billions of years ago in epic fashion, dispersing matter across the billions of light-years that the universe spans. That material eventually coalesced into the stars, planets, black holes, galaxies, and the other celestial objects that populate our skies. One such explanation is found in *Universe—The Definitive Visual Guide*, © 2005, DK Publishing, New York, New York:

"Time, space, energy, and matter are all thought to have come into existence 13.7 billion years ago, in the event called the Big Bang. In its first moments, the universe was infinitely dense, unimaginably hot, and contained pure energy. But within a tiny fraction

3

of a second, a vast number of fundamental particles had appeared, created out of energy as the universe cooled. Within a few hundred thousand years, these particles had combined to form the first atoms. Physicists believe that gravity split from the other forces of nature . . ."

There is more to the explanation, but these segments highlight factors that critics note contradict some basic laws of physics as well as logic.

Matter and energy cannot simply appear out of nowhere in time and space. If there was a *"Big Bang,"* where did the stuff that went "bang" come from, and what made it go bang? Likewise, we would need to conclude that the forces that govern the universe just appeared. Gravity is a major stumbling block for Big Bang theorists. Nobody knows its provenance. (Google the question if you doubt this). Similarly, where do such things as magnetism, light, and the forces that bind together the subatomic particles that compose atoms originate? We can measure them, observe them, and control them to some extent. We can fill entire chalkboards with equations that describe their interactions. But how did they come into existence?

Consider what we know about the universe through marvels such as the Hubble Telescope. If the earth were the size of a golf ball, our sun would be fifteen feet in diameter. The second-largest star discovered to date, *Canis Majoris,* would have a diameter as tall as Mt. Everest—29,000 feet. The moon is suspended in space by centrifugal force balanced by gravity. Yet we are asked to believe by secularists that the cosmic ballet in which the universe dances just came about by chance. Psalm 19:1 reminds us— *"the heavens declare the Glory of God."*

Similarly, the notion that all life on earth today evolved from a single cell that appeared millions of years ago by a random chance event that brought together the substances which comprise a cell, requires a greater leap of faith than believing in the existence of a Creator-God. Author and atheist-turned-Christian Lee Strobel concluded: *"To continue in atheism, I would need to believe that nothing produces everything, non-life produces life, randomness produces*

4

fine-tuning, chaos produces information, unconsciousness produces consciousness, and non-reason produces reason. I simply don't have that much faith."

Before it could evolve, that first cell postulated by evolutionists had to reproduce. Cellular reproduction requires pre-existing instructions embedded within the cell. Aside from the chance combining of the chemicals required to form the cell, how was that microscopic program devised that told the cell it had to divide, and then controlled the process?

Let's get more specific. Geophysicist and college professor Dr. Stephen C. Meyer (Ph.D. in Philosophy of Science, Cambridge), has authored three books on mankind's origins. He notes in the April 2021 issue of *Decision* magazine:

"Since the 1960s, further discoveries made clear that the digital information in DNA and its cellular neighbor, RNA, is only part of a complex information processing system—an advanced form of nanotechnology that both mirrors and exceeds our own in its complexity, design logic, and information density."

Most well-informed scientists favor a view known as "Irreducible Complexity," which concludes that the complexity of life mandates that it was originally designed rather than resulting from some chance occurrence and random mutations over millions of years. Dr. Walter L. Bradley, (Ph.D., Material Science), an expert in polymers and thermodynamics, has written or collaborated in five books or articles on the origins of life. Interviewed by Lee Strobel for Strobel's book, *The Case for Faith*, Bradley explains:

"...the mathematical odds of assembling a living organism are so astronomical that nobody still believes random chance accounts for the origins of life. ... If you took all the carbon in the universe and put it on earth, allowed it to chemically react at the most rapid rate possible, and left it for billions of years, the odds of creating just one functional protein molecule would be one chance in a 10 with 60 zeroes after it."

[$1/10^{60}$] In my view, this equates to mathematical impossibility.

Does it not seem more likely that the universe, earth, and all life on earth were created by an all-powerful God who eternally exists outside of space and time?

Two thousand years ago, the apostle Paul wrote: *"For ever since the world was created, people have seen the earth and sky. Through everything God made, they can clearly see his invisible qualities—his eternal power and divine nature. So they have no excuse for not knowing God."* (Romans 1:20, NLT.)

My eyes and reason convince me God is real. You will have to decide how you choose to answer this question. Consider this: if there is no God and the universe and life came into being by chance events, then what is the purpose of our existence? But if we are created beings, then, (1) we have a purpose in life; (2) there is a creator superior to us whom we need to acknowledge; and, (3) we have value to the One who created us.

What Is The Bible? Why Should It Alone Be Trusted?

In addition to the Christian Bible, (hereafter *"the Bible"*), other books such as the Koran, The Book of Mormon, and the version of the Bible followed by Jehovah's Witnesses, purport to be the sole source of God's word. They all contradict the Bible, as well as each other, in so many ways that only one such book can claim that honor.

The Bible, and Biblical Christianity, are unique among the major world religions. The Bible is based on God reaching down to mankind, while other religions are based on mankind reaching up by its efforts to God, typically requiring people to do some undefined amount of *"good"* works to get to heaven. But none of those other religions can precisely define the nature and quantities of the good works we must perform to be sure we'll reach heaven. Perhaps most striking, Biblical Christianity is the only faith whose founder, Jesus Christ, was raised from the dead by Divine power, witnessed by hundreds of people. Jesus Christ is still alive in heaven seated at the right hand of God. The Bible contains multiple passages documenting His appearances after God raised Him from the grave, including eye-witness accounts. These include:

• Two women (Matthew 28:9-10);

• Mary Magdalene (John 20:11-18);

• The Apostle Peter (Luke 24:34; Mark 16:7);

• Two travelers, one named Cleopas, on the road to Emmaus (Luke 24:13-31);

• The eleven original disciples remaining after Judas committed suicide out of guilt for betraying Jesus, and to other disciples (Luke 24:36-49; John 20:19-23);

• The previous group on three other occasions (John 20:24-29; Matthew 28:16-20; Acts 1:6-9; Luke 24:50-51);

• Seven of the disciples (1 John 21:1-4.)

1 Corinthians 15:5-8, written by the apostle Paul, who also had an encounter, summarizes them and adds to the ones listed above:

"...he appeared to Cephas [Peter], and then to the Twelve. After that, he appeared to more than five hundred of the brothers and sisters at the same time, most of whom are still living, though some have fallen asleep. Then he appeared to James, then to all the apostles, and last, of all, he appeared to me, as to one abnormally born."

There is more independent verification of the Bible, such as the Dead Sea Scrolls and the historic works of Josephus than any other foundational book of faith. It is not one book written by one author in one sitting. Rather, it is a collection of sixty-six books written over 1,500 years by some forty different authors. It is considered as God's true word and infallible.

The Bible is divided into two parts. The Old Testament traces the time from the creation of the heavens and the earth through a time about four hundred years before the birth of Jesus Christ. The large majority of its text is devoted to the inception of the nation of Israel as a distinct and separate people group, and Israel's saga and relationship with God spanning many centuries. The New Testament traces the time from the birth of Jesus to a point about one hundred years after His death. The last chapter, known as the Book of Revelation, describes the end times of the Earth as we know it, culminating in a massive war between good and evil forces, and including the final judgment of mankind by God.

Among the many factors that support the reliability and validity of the Bible, I will reference one, which *prima facia* is convincing. There are some three hundred prophecies (foretelling of future events) in the Old Testament forecasting events that occurred hundreds of years later. This is mathematically impossible unless each prophecy was directed and inspired by the God who has control of all things and caused those prophecies to be fulfilled.

Evolution vs. creation remains a hotly-debated topic. Evidence continues to mount that counters the theory of evolution. For an in-depth look at this subject, websites such as *creation.com* are instructive. The global flood described in Genesis which covered the entire earth with water to a depth twenty-three feet above the top of the highest mountain, and the powerful rushing subsidence of all that water, can account for many geologic features and fossil deposits that evolutionists claim took millions of years to form. If you've ever carried a five-gallon container of water, consider how much weight the Biblical flood waters would bring to bear upon the surface of the earth.

My study and reflection, including a review of the Koran, the Book of Mormon, and some comparisons of the form of the Bible followed by Jehovah's Witness adherents, lead me to conclude that the Christian Bible contains God's truth. Every person should soberly engage in a search for the truth. The Bible reminds us that the truth shall set us free.

Getting To Know God

It was once said that most of mankind's troubles stem from an improper picture and understanding of God. To fully appreciate the Bible, we need to know God's attributes, although our mortal minds cannot comprehend Him. Theologian A.W. Tozer, in his book *The Knowledge of the Holy*, discusses the attributes denoted below. Tozer suggests that it is both inaccurate and disrespectful to ask, *"What is God 'like,'"* for He has no equal in all the universe. Nothing compares to Him, for He is above all.

When we try to describe God, we are limited to using human words that produce human analogies, resemblances, and actions to depict One whose person and works exist on an unimaginably higher plane outside of space and time that is simply impossible for us to comprehend and envision.

• God is omnipotent.

He holds all power.

"In the beginning, God created the heavens and the earth." (Genesis 1:1.)

"Through Him (the Word) all things were made; without Him, nothing was made that has been made." (John 1:3.)

• God is sovereign.

He (not us) rules His entire creation.

"…The Most High is sovereign over all kingdoms on earth…" (Daniel 4:25.)

• God is omnipresent.

He surrounds creation; there is no place beyond Him for anything to be; there is no place anywhere to hide from Him; He knows our innermost thoughts. (Psalm 139.)

• God is transcendent.

He exists outside of space and time. He is so far above human thought that we cannot conceive of Him.

"For my thoughts are not your thoughts, neither are your ways my ways. As the heavens are higher than the earth, so are my ways higher than your ways, and my thoughts than your thoughts." (Isaiah 55:8-9.)

• God is omniscient.

He possesses all knowledge; He cannot be taught anything, and indeed could never have a "teacher."

"Who can fathom the mind of the Lord, or instruct as His counselor? Whom did the Lord consult to enlighten Him, and who taught Him the right way?" (Isaiah 40:13-14.)

• God is infinite.

He is limitless, an impossible thing for a limited (human) mind to grasp. He cannot be measured, as measurements have limits.

"Can you probe the limits of the Almighty?" (Job 11:7.)

"I am the Alpha and the Omega, the first and the last, the beginning and the end." (Revelation 22:12.)

• God is eternal.

He exists outside of time. He has no past or future. He has always existed and will always exist. He has no deadlines or time limits in which to accomplish His will. Our entire lives are enslaved by time. We count our seconds, minutes, hours, days, and years until our mortal end. We cannot grasp the idea of eternity.

"...From everlasting to everlasting, you are God...a thousand years in your sight are like a day that has just gone by..." (Psalm 90:2, 4.)

"For God so loved the world that He gave His one and only Son, that whoever believes in Him shall not perish but have eternal life." (John 3:16.)

• God is self-sufficient.

All created living things need food, water, and air to survive. God needs nothing. Rather, He is the provider of the needs for all the things He created. In Him, the universe is sustained.

"The Father has life in Himself." (John 5:26.)

"And in Him, all things hold together." (Colossians 1:17.)

• God possesses all wisdom.

In our pride, we think of ourselves as wise. Sometimes we think we know better than God, and try to run our lives contrary to His counsel. How has that worked out for mankind?

"The fear (awesome respect) of the Lord is the beginning of wisdom." (Psalm 111:10.)

"The foolishness of God is wiser than human wisdom." (1 Corinthians 1:25.)

• God is self-existent.

He has no origin. Only created things have an origin (and a creator). Our minds can't understand this, for everything in our world has some sort of origin.

"He is before all things, and in Him, all things hold together." (Colossians 1:17.)

"Moses said to God, 'Suppose I go to the Israelites and say to them,' 'The God of your fathers has sent me to you," and they ask me, 'What is His name?' "Then what shall I tell them?" God said to Moses, 'I Am Who I Am.'" (Exodus 13:14.)

• God is Holy.

His holiness sets him above all others. *"Who will not fear you, Lord, and bring glory to your name? For you alone are holy. ..."* (Revelation 15:4.)

These attributes set God far above and beyond mortal mankind. Contemplating just one should leave us in awe and wonder. But to consider that God possesses all of them should leave us not only speechless but fully confident that He indeed has the power to create the universe and everything in it.

"He sits enthroned above the circle of the earth, and its people are like grasshoppers. Lift up your eyes and look to the heavens: Who created all of these? The Lord is the everlasting God, the creator of the ends of the earth." (Isaiah 40:22; 26; 28.)

Yet God has another set of attributes that intersect with humankind. Tozer notes that God is full of grace, mercy, love, patience, justice, goodness, and faithfulness. Despite our shortcomings, we are not left without common ground to form a relationship with God.

Making Sense Of Our Chaotic World And Uncertain Future

To understand the teachings in the Bible, as well as our present circumstances, we need to revisit mankind's journey from the time of creation. To complete our understanding, we need to know what the Bible tells us about the Last Days when mankind will face epic disasters, tribulation, and final judgment that will determine every person's eternal destiny. It may be tempting to ignore such discomforting topics or to invoke our denial defense that they are too far-fetched to be true. In the end, truth and reality will still be waiting for us. We can only postpone our inevitable meeting with them.

On the other hand, perhaps you are one who wisely stores up food, water, and other physical necessities in case of a possible disaster. If the Bible presents the truth, however uncomfortable some of it may be, doesn't it make sense to at least consider making the same sort of preparations for your soul? You will find that there is no need to fear the future or death if you make the right choices.

The first verses of the first book of the Bible, Genesis, describe God's acts of creation as follows: *"In the beginning, God created the heavens and the earth."* (Genesis 1:1.) The successive steps of creation are recounted, as we see God create the waters of the earth, the plant and animal life, and the pinnacle of His creation—us, mankind. Genesis 1:26 states:

"Then God said, 'Let us make mankind in our image, in our likeness, so that they may rule over the fish in the sea, the birds in the sky, over the livestock and all the wild animals, and over all the creatures that move along the ground.'"

God declared his creation *"very good."*

God's original intent was for humanity to live forever in fellowship with Him. The first two humans He created—Adam and Eve—were given a

15

garden to live in, with everything they needed to sustain themselves, including a tree in the middle of the garden called the tree of life, which provided the means for them to live forever. Adam had only one food restriction. God commanded: *"You may freely eat the fruit of every tree in the garden—except the tree of the knowledge of good and evil. If you eat its fruit, you are sure to die."* (Genesis 2:16-17, NLT.) (See generally, Genesis 2:8-17.)

God gave Adam and Eve free will, including the choice to obey or disobey Him. Their choice in this matter led to the loss of eternal paradise, not only for them but also for all their descendants throughout history, including us.

We don't know how long Adam and Eve lived in that innocent paradise before creation was ruined, but Genesis later tells us that they, and by extension, all of humanity born after them, could have lived in an eternal relationship with God, had Adam and Eve simply obeyed that one simple command.

The third chapter of Genesis moves forward to the defining moment of our present existence and reveals our unfortunate natures. A serpent appears in the garden without any explanation of who or what he is. (The last book of the Bible, Revelation, identifies the serpent as *"...that ancient serpent, who is the devil"* (Satan). (Revelation 20:2.) Satan's role in our present circumstances will be elaborated upon shortly.)

The serpent and Eve have a chat (Genesis 3:1-7.)

"Now the serpent was more crafty than any of the wild animals the Lord God had made. He said to the woman, 'Did God really say, You must not eat from any tree in the garden?'"

"The woman said to the serpent, 'We may eat from the fruit of the trees in the garden, but God did say, You must not eat fruit from the tree that is in the middle of the garden, and you must not touch it, or you will die.'"

16

Eve is aware that there is forbidden fruit, but she seems a little confused about the specifics of the prohibition.

"You will not certainly die," the serpent said to the woman. "For God knows that when you eat from it your eyes will be opened, and you will be like God, knowing good and evil."

The serpent responds with a half-truth combined with another lie, sweetened by the implication that God is holding back something good from her and Adam. The serpent dangles more bait by claiming that they will be like God if they eat the forbidden fruit. The latter enticement is not only a complete lie, it is at the heart of most of our troubles in life, both individually and corporately as nations. The Bible warns us, there is none like God; we ignore this at our peril. Those familiar with the story know what comes next.

"When the woman saw that the fruit of the tree was good for food and pleasing to the eye, and also desirable for gaining wisdom, she took some and ate it. She also gave some to her husband, who was with her, and he ate it. Then the eyes of both of them were opened, and they realized they were naked; so they sewed fig leaves together and made coverings for themselves."

The consequences of this primal act of disobedience, often called the original sin, are recounted in Genesis 3:14-24. Some were immediate and fell upon Adam and Eve. Unfortunately for mankind, the long-term consequences infected every generation born from that time forward and will continue to plague mankind until the end times decreed by God. Our sin natures inherited from Adam and Eve are like a genetic defect carried by every person on earth which we are powerless by ourselves to eradicate.

Adam and Eve immediately experienced shame and guilt. Before their disobedience, they were innocent children, heedless of being unclothed among all the unclothed creatures of creation. In an instant, they were transported from a perfect creation to one where evil gained a foothold and began its reign. They knew they had done something very wrong.

17

When God confronted them with their disobedience, their responses were classic. Thousands of years later, we still use the same lame excuses to justify our wrongful actions. Here is the standard dialog repeated in households every day when children are caught doing something wrong (as well as in the halls of government when elected officials are caught in their misdeeds.)

When God challenged Adam, Adam replied: *"The woman you put here with me—she gave me some fruit from the tree, and I ate it."*

God then said to the woman, *"What is this you have done?"*

The woman (Eve) answered: *"The serpent deceived me and I ate."* (Genesis 3:12-13.)

The first blame game dates back to the time of creation. It's all her/his/someone else's fault. The serpent apparently had nobody else to blame.

The long-term consequences for the serpent and Adam and Eve are then delineated. The serpent is condemned to crawl on its belly and eat dust all of its life. And of significance for us today, enmity ("positive, active mutual hatred and ill will," per the Merriam-Webster dictionary) is put between the serpent's offspring and the woman's.

This pronouncement thousands of years ago marked the beginning of the earthly battle between good and evil which will continue until the end times for mankind.

To round out the consequences for women, Eve and the generations of women to follow were condemned to suffer severe pains in childbearing and labor in giving birth. God added, *"Your desire shall be for your husband, and he will rule over you."*

As for Adam, as well as subsequent generations, God declared:

"Cursed is the ground because of you; through painful toil, you will eat food from it all the days of your life. It will produce thorns and thistles for you, and you will eat the plants of the field. By the sweat of your brow, you will eat your food until you return to the ground."

Doesn't that sound like our typical work week?

The final consequence of Adam's sin condemned all of mankind to death. "And The Lord God said, *'The man has now become like one of us, knowing good and evil. He must not be allowed to reach out his hand and take also from the tree of life and eat and* **live forever.***'"* (emphasis supplied). God then banished Adam from the garden and blocked his access to the tree of life by placing an angel with flaming swords in front of it. (Genesis 3:22-24.)

In addition to physical death, Adam's disobedience ushered spiritual death into the world, severing mankind's spiritual connection to God. But in his great mercy, God has provided us the means to restore our relationship with Him. Don't lose hope!

The fall in the garden cursed mankind with pain, evil, turmoil, and death. Too harsh a result? Only if we try to place ourselves on a plane equal to, or maybe above, God. Isn't that where Adam and Eve went wrong? And what about Satan?

Our Invisible Enemies

There is a fair consensus that Satan, or the devil, was once an angel of the highest order in heaven who rebelled against God, perhaps thinking he was capable of being equal with God. Satan was cast out of heaven together with other disobedient angels who were his followers. Angels, who are mentioned throughout the Bible, are created beings who differ in terms of abilities and natures from humans, and by implication seem to predate the creation of mankind. Mankind is made a little lower than angels (see Psalm 8:4-6.)

Many of us choose to disbelieve the existence of the devil, or evil. This is a fatal error in judgment and leaves the disbeliever an easy prey for him, susceptible to his lies and deceit. Lies can control our lives as easily as the truth. Is there any coherent explanation for random massacres and school shootings other than evil at work? What about the belief that there is a God who will be extremely happy with us if we slaughter and behead certain other people?

It is critical to know what the Bible says about Satan. Although God is all-powerful and Satan is subject to God's ultimate authority, Satan holds a great deal of power over the events and people on the earth as evidenced in several verses:

John 12:31 characterizes Satan as *"...the prince of this world (earth)..."*

During an encounter between Jesus and Satan in which Satan tries to tempt Jesus to abandon God, Satan took Jesus.

"...to a high place and showed him in an instant all the kingdoms of the world. And he said to him, 'I will give you all their authority and splendor; it has been given to me, and I can give it to anyone I want to. If you worship me, it will all be yours.'" (Luke 4:5-7.)

1 John 5:18-19 (NLT) tells us:

"We know that God's children do not make a practice of sinning, for God's Son holds them securely, and the evil one cannot touch them. We know that we are children of God and that the world around us is under the control of the evil one."

We have a powerful enemy whom we cannot see, for our battle is an invisible one, waged primarily in the mind. The apostle Paul describes it in Ephesians 6:12:

"For our struggle is not against flesh and blood, but against the rulers, against the authorities, against the powers of this dark world, and against the spiritual forces of evil in the heavenly realms."

Grasping this requires a major shift in thinking for the Western mind. In our culture, the idea of an invisible realm inhabited by spirit beings is mostly relegated to fairy tales and movies. However, it is very real. As you contemplate this, are you thinking, *"this is a bunch of b.s.?"* If so, you are experiencing the very battle for our minds that Paul describes. Where did that thought originate, or any others that urge you to reject the Bible? We can't see the wind, atoms, or germs but they are real.

The Bible makes it clear that there is a spirit realm in which evil spirits dwell, and we are warned in no uncertain terms to avoid any contact with the occult. God's words to the young nation of Israel ring true today. Deuteronomy 18:10-12:

"Let no one be found among you who sacrifices their son or daughter in the fire (child sacrifice was practiced among the pagan nations in Old Testament times), who practices divination or sorcery, interprets omens, engages in witchcraft, or casts spells, or who is a medium or spiritist or who consults the dead. Anyone who does these things is detestable to the Lord;..."

Seemingly innocent diversions like ouija boards and tarot cards play in these dark realms; mind-altering drugs would also seem to dwell there.

Likewise, we are warned of false spirits that claim to come from God. If you intend to move forward with what the Bible teaches, it is critical to learn how to distinguish truth from the deceptions promoted by such spirits. Become intimately familiar with what the Bible teaches. 2 Corinthians 10:5 tells us: *"…take captive every thought to make it obedient to Christ."*

Satan's nature and methods are described in other verses.

John 8:44 declares: *"…He was a murderer from the beginning, not holding to the truth, for there is no truth in him. When he lies, he speaks his native language, for he is a liar and the father of lies."*

2 Corinthians 11:14 instructs us: *"…Satan himself masquerades as an angel of light."*

Satan cannot force us to do anything against our will. But we are susceptible to his lies and distortions that lead us astray and prompt us to satisfy our fallen natures as opposed to doing what we know is right.

Our minds are the battlefield. Every word we speak, every action we take, everything we believe to be true or not true, begins with a thought or series of thoughts. It's easy to let our thoughts run free and to act on them without stopping to consider where they originate, especially when they are driven by emotions. Think about what you're thinking about, and where it comes from.

The Rocky Road From The Garden And The First Murder

After Adam and Eve's expulsion from the garden, mankind began its agonizing journey. Along the way, our rebellious natures have kept us from reconciling our relationship with our Creator. When we look at the murders, the wars, the hate, the suffering, and diseases that continue to plague us, we may wonder why God permits this if He loves us. Our life on Earth was not intended to be like this, and at one time long ago, it wasn't. While God may have the power to stop all our suffering, He didn't start it. Mankind did, and we continue to reap the consequences of incredibly bad human decisions that began thousands of years before the birth of Jesus. But take heart that it will end one day for all who choose the path God has provided us for escape.

Adam and Eve had several children. Two of the earliest were sons, Cain and Abel. Cain worked the soil while Abel cared for livestock. It was the practice to offer sacrifices to God to atone for sin. The best of whatever was produced—crops or livestock—was expected to be offered. Cain became angry and jealous because God accepted an offering from Abel, but rejected Cain's offering. Cain offered some of what he grew, while Abel offered fat portions from some of the firstborn of his flock. Abel offered the best and most valuable of the fruits of his labor, while Cain likely offered something of inferior quality.

After that rejection,

"...Cain was very angry, and his face was downcast. Then the Lord said to Cain, 'Why are you angry? Why is your face downcast? If you do what is right, will you not be accepted? But if you do not do what is right, sin is crouching at your door; it desires to have you, but you must rule over it." (Genesis 4:5-7.)

Cain made his choice. He let his anger control him, and he killed Abel. Has human nature changed since then?

25

Sin and sacrifice are introduced in these passages as central concepts that define (1) our fallen relationship with God (sin), and (2) the means ordained to atone for sin (sacrifice). The original readership for whom Genesis was written likely understood these concepts, as they were integral parts of their lives. For us, today's readers, their importance and explanation can only be fully understood by reading and studying the rest of the Bible. A summary here must suffice.

What Is Sin?

Scholars have delineated three types of sin:

Original sin, resulting from Adam's disobedience to God in eating the forbidden fruit. This is the systemic, inborn sin that affects and corrupts every person, every descendant, every generation born of Adam and Eve. It is akin to a genetic defect that infects every member of the human race who will ever live. Romans 3:23 states that all have sinned and fall short of the glory of God.

Imputed sin stems from violations of the law handed down by God to govern the lives of the nation of Israel. Many of us are familiar with the Ten Commandments which prohibit such things as idol worship, murder, lying, and theft. These eventually grew into some 600 laws that governed Israel. Disobedience is again the key element.

Personal sin concerns our everyday conduct. Malice, anger, self-centeredness, sexual immorality, greed, and other behaviors that violate the righteous lifestyle God has directed us to live are prime examples. Satisfying our fleshly desires or obtaining a personal gain, without regard to the propriety of the means used or consequences to others and ourselves, typically motivate these actions.

Sin is not measured by comparing one person's conduct to another's, for the Bible tells us, *"All have sinned and fall short of the glory (the absolute Holiness) of God"* who is without sin. Nothing tainted by sin can be tolerated in God's presence. Romans 6:23 tells us that the wage of even one sin is death.

Sacrifice

The practice of making sacrifices to God appears first with the story of Cain and Abel but receives scant mention afterward. It appears again with Noah and the story of the flood. It can be inferred that the practice was present to some extent since the time of the first humans. It rose to significant importance with the inception of the nation of Israel.

Offerings or sacrifices to God to atone for sins, both personal and corporate, were a central part of God's worship directives to the Israelites. Those rituals were complex and elaborate, described at length in the Bible. Many involved the killing of animals, sacrificing them on an altar.

The necessity of a blood sacrifice to atone for sins was deeply embedded in the life of Israel for all of its generations. Leviticus 17:11 defines the significance of that sacrifice:

"For the life of a creature is in the blood, and I have given it to you to make atonement for yourselves on the altar; it is the blood that makes atonement for one's life."

Hebrews 9:22, found in the New Testament, reiterates:

"...without the shedding of blood, there is no forgiveness."

Noah And The Flood

Adam's descendants began to greatly increase in numbers but continued mankind's pattern of choosing evil over good. Although those early people acknowledged God's existence, they chose a murderous and immoral lifestyle. God's patience with humanity after the first murder lasted about 1,600 years (as calculated by myself according to the successive genealogies given in Genesis 5. Some scholars have differing views on the very early time frames of events. The *Zondervan Quest Study Bible* makes no attempts to assign dates to any events before the birth of Abram, the father of the Jewish nation, Israel, which it places at about 2,166 BC.)

Genesis 6:5-8 relate God's reaction:

"The Lord saw how great the wickedness of the human race had become on earth, and that every inclination of the thoughts of the human heart was only evil all the time. The Lord regretted that he had made human beings on the earth, and his heart was deeply troubled. So the Lord said, 'I will wipe from the face of the earth the human race I have created—and with them the animals, the birds, and the creatures that move along the ground—for I regret that I have made them.' But Noah found favor in the eyes of the Lord."

What distinguished Noah? Genesis 6:9: *"…Noah was a righteous man, blameless among the people of his time, and he walked faithfully with God."* God's mercy was granted to eight people: Noah, his three sons, and their wives.

God directed Noah to build an ark (boat) 450 feet long, 75 feet wide, and 45 feet high, and to bring aboard his entire family, seven breeding pairs (male and female) of every kind of bird and clean animal, and one breeding pair of every kind of unclean animal, together with food, to escape a great flood that God would bring upon the earth.

Noah's three sons were born after Noah was 500 years old; the flood occurred when Noah was 600 years old. We aren't told how long it took to build the ark; estimates run from fifty-five to seventy-five years. If God told any of us to build a boat approaching the size of an ocean-going vessel out of wood using only hand tools, to escape an upcoming flood, would we have the faith to devote over fifty years to the task?

When Noah, his family, and the animals were safely aboard, God brought flood waters for forty days that covered the entire earth, rising twenty-three feet above the highest mountain (Genesis 7:19.) Every living thing that moved on land, and all mankind, perished. The waters covered the earth for 150 days and then began to recede. The occupants of the ark were on board for about a year before the waters receded to the point where they could leave the ark. God commanded Noah and his family to go forth and multiply, to repopulate the earth. Mankind was given another chance to get it right. As of today, how's that working out for us? (The complete account of Noah and the flood can be found in Genesis 6:9— 7:23).

Another Big Stumble

When Noah and his family left the ark, Noah built an altar and sacrificed a burnt offering to God of some of the animals and birds from the ark (theologians think it likely that some animal offspring were born on the ark.) God vowed to never again destroy the earth by a flood. God also said in his heart, *"Never again will I curse the ground because of humans, even though every inclination of the human heart is evil from childhood..."* (Genesis 8:21.)

Noah and his sons honored God's command to be fruitful and fill the earth. Many tribes and nations having a common language were formed by their descendants, spreading over a large area (see Genesis 10.) But after a time, a great mass of them gathered and settled on a plain in Shinar. There, they determined to build a city with a great tower (the Tower of Babel) that reached the heavens, to make a name for themselves and, to avoid being scattered over the face of the earth. In other words, they decided to do things their way rather than God's. Some analysts think the tower was intended to provide a way for a deity to come down to enter his temple to be worshipped.

God was not pleased with this disobedience and show of pride. As Genesis 11:5-8 recount,

"...the Lord came down to see the city and the tower the people were building. The Lord said, 'If as one people speaking the same language they have begun to do this, then nothing they plan to do will be impossible for them. Come, let us go down and confuse their language so they will not understand each other.' So the Lord scattered them from there all over the earth, and they stopped building the city."

Commentators opine that the phrase *"nothing will be impossible"* is not meant literally, but rather to indicate that this mass of people had the potential to do a great deal of evil when united around a common improper purpose. The same dynamic has continued to work throughout history where evil intent unites a group of people capable of carrying it out.

33

Dying To Live

34

Setting The Stage For God's Final Act

Almost 300 years after the flood, around 2,166 BC, a man named Abram was born. In Genesis 12, without any background story as to why, God spoke to Abram and instructed him to leave his country, his father's household, and the security of a comfortable living, to go to a place God would later show Abram, with some amazing promises:

"I will make you into a great nation, and I will bless you; I will make your name great, and you will be a blessing. I will bless those who bless you, and whoever curses you I will curse, and all peoples on earth will be blessed through you." (Genesis 12:2-3.)

Abram continued to walk with God. As the years passed, he and his wife, Sarai, remained childless. God came to him again and promised that he would have a son who would be his heir and that his offspring would be as numerous as the stars in the sky. *"Abram believed the Lord, and he credited it to him as righteousness."* (Genesis 15:6.)

But after ten years had passed and no children were born of Sarai, she gave her servant Hagar to Abram to have a child with. Shocking as this is to our present sensibilities and customs, it was a common cultural practice at that time. Childbearing was one of the most important duties of a wife.

When Hagar became pregnant, she chided Sarai, who in anger mistreated Hagar, driving Hagar from Abram's household into the wilderness. An angel of the Lord appeared to Hagar and directed Hagar to return to Abram's household, telling Hagar that she would bear a son to be named Ishmael who would have too many descendants to count, and who would be *"...a wild donkey of a man; his hand will be against everyone and everyone's hand against him, and he will live in hostility toward all his brothers."* (Genesis 16:12.)

Hagar returned to Abram's household, submitted to Sarai, and gave birth to Ishmael when Abram was eighty-six. If Abram and Sarai thought this was the son God had promised, they were to find out God had something else in mind. When Ishmael was 13, God appeared to Abram again and made a covenant to Abram that set the course of human history, and the Middle East in particular. God promised that Sarai, who was almost ninety, would bear Abram a son to be named Isaac within the year. Abram would be the father (and Sarai the mother) of many nations, and kings; and Abram's descendants would possess the whole land known as Canaan as an everlasting possession. God added that His covenant would be with Isaac. He renamed Abram as Abraham and Sarai as Sarah.

Abraham asked God if He would also bless Ishmael. God affirmed the promise made to Hagar, saying that Ishmael would be the father of many, including twelve *"rulers."* However, God reiterated that His covenant would be with Isaac.

The saga of Abraham and his descendants fills the remainder of the Old Testament, covering a period of about two thousand years. The descendants of Abraham and Isaac are the Jews, the nation of Israel, God's chosen people. As for Ishmael's descendants, twelve sons are named in the Bible. Each of them became the ruler of a tribe, and *"...they lived in hostility toward all the tribes related to them,"* just as God foretold. (Genesis 25:18.)

It is widely considered that Ishmael's descendants are the Arabs of today, who have battled against Israel since the inception of the tribes formed by those descendants, just as God said. That conflict has spread to the rest of the world with the establishment of Islam as a predominant religion in the Middle East about 1,400 years ago. Abraham and Sarah's impatience in waiting for God's timing for them to have a son together caused them to take matters into their own hands, setting in motion the forces that grew into the terrorism we face today.

Many consider the continuous existence and survival of the Jews for some 4,000 years, and the creation of the country of Israel in 1948, despite the efforts of multiple empires and nations far more powerful to eradicate them, as proof of God's existence. Their remarkable history exemplifies

God's total dominion over His earth and also illustrates how mankind's sinful human nature and stubborn pride can keep us from enjoying the blessings and benefits of walking in God's paths rather than our own. More importantly, the fate of all mankind is inseparably woven together with that of Israel. There is a very good reason why Israel and the Middle East are always in the news. We need to pay attention to what unfolds there.

The early generations of Israel migrated to Egypt, the dominant regional power, to escape a famine. After a period of peaceful coexistence, the Egyptians became alarmed at the rapid population growth of the Israelites. Fearful of being overtaken in numbers and power by the Israelites, Egypt's military subdued Israel.

When God made his covenant with Abraham, he told Abraham this:

"Know for certain that for four hundred years your descendants will be strangers in a country not their own and that they will be enslaved and mistreated there. But I will punish the nation they serve as slaves, and afterward they will come out with great possessions." (Genesis 14:13-14.)

Just as God foretold, several generations after Abraham lived, Israel was driven into 400 years of Egyptian captivity and slavery.

After four centuries of brutal oppression, the nation of Israel cried out to God to free it from the Egyptians. God heard their cry and chose a man named Moses to lead them out of Egypt. Moses approached Egypt's leader, Pharoah, with a demand to free the Israelites. Moses warned Pharoah that refusal would bring suffering upon Egypt by the hand of the God of Israel. (In contrast to Israel's worship of the one true God, Egypt and the other pagan cultures in those times worshipped multiple gods and man-made idols.)

Pharaoh refused, and Egypt suffered a series of ten plagues sent by God, each worse than the previous one. Crops were devoured by locusts;

festering boils erupted on people and animals; hail rained down, killing people and animals; insects plagued the land. After each plague, Moses repeated his demand and was repeatedly refused.

The final plague took the lives of the firstborn sons of all the Egyptians, including the Pharoah's son. Before that plague arrived, God instructed the Israelites to smear the blood of lambs over the door frames of their homes. The plague passed over the Israelites' homes, sparing their children. This *"Passover"* is observed annually as an important Jewish religious day.

After this plague, Pharoah relented and allowed the Israelites to leave Egypt. On their way out, the fearful Egyptians showered the Israelites with gold, silver, and clothing, all as foretold by God to Abraham generations earlier.

Moving Day

Exodus 12:37 tells us that there were about *"…600,000 men on foot, besides women and children…"* who left Egypt. Estimates conclude that there were over one million people, plus their livestock and possessions.

This monumental nation made its way through the desert until it came upon an impassable barrier, the Red Sea. Meanwhile, Pharaoh was having second thoughts about losing his entire free labor force and sent his army and charioteers after the Israelites to bring them back. Trapped between the sea and the Egyptian army, the Israelites railed against Moses, certain that they would be killed. Even after seeing God's repeated miracles that had freed them from Egypt, they lacked the faith that He would deliver them.

Moses prayed to God and was told to stretch out his staff over the sea. God then parted the sea, allowing the entire nation to pass through on dry ground to the other side. When the Egyptian army attempted pursuit through the parted waters, God collapsed the waters over the army, drowning it.

Three months after leaving Egypt, the Israelites encamped in the Sinai Desert near Mount Sinai after defeating the peoples known as Amalekites, with God's power bringing victory. There, God began shaping Israel to become a nation set apart and distinct from all others, devoted to and worshipping him alone. The pagan nations that populated the Middle East at that time, including Egypt, engaged in the worship of multiple gods, idols, and practices abhorrent to God such as using temple prostitutes in their religious rites and even child sacrifice. Israel was intended to stand in stark contrast. (The term *"nation"* in those times did not so much signify a geographic territory with distinct boundaries as it does today, but rather a sizable group of people who may have been nomadic with distinct common characteristics such as ancestry, race, customs, or clothing, similar to Native American tribes.)

God called Moses to a series of meetings with Him on Mount Sinai to set forth His laws to govern Israel in all of its life practices and worship from that time forward. His first instructions to Moses were to tell the Israelites this:

"You yourselves have seen what I did to Egypt, and how I carried you on eagles' wings and brought you to myself. Now if you obey me fully and keep my covenant, then out of all nations you will be my treasured possession. Although the whole earth is mine, you will be for me a kingdom of priests and a holy nation." (Exodus 19:4-6.)

God's covenant reiterated his promise to bless Abraham's descendants, but importantly, Israel was required to obey God and keep His covenants if they were to continue to receive God's blessings. The rest of mankind was left to its own devices.

Moses returned from one of his meetings with God carrying the written set of laws known as the Ten Commandments, which form the moral basis of many of our laws today. The first two forbid the people from having any other god before God Himself, and from making any man-made idols to worship, emphasizing Israel's separation from the pagan cultures around it.

Another such meeting kept Moses away for forty days.

"When the people saw that Moses was so long in coming down from the mountain, they gathered around Aaron (Moses' brother,) and said, 'Come, make us gods who will go before us. As for this fellow Moses who brought us up from Egypt, we don't know what happened to him.'" (Exodus 32:1.)

Ponder this. The Israelites had just witnessed ten severe plagues brought by God against Egypt, the Passover, the parting of the Red Sea, the food and water provided for over a million of them in a desert that had no food or water, and a military victory, all brought about by the hand of God who had just commanded them not to make idols! It took only forty days

40

without their leader keeping them focused on God for them to abandon God.

Aaron gave in to the people's pressure, rather than standing firm on God's commands. He had the people bring him their gold earrings and fashioned them with a tool into an idol in the shape of a calf. The people said, *"...These are your gods, Israel, who brought you up out of Egypt."* (Exodus 32:4.) Aaron built an altar in front of the calf and called for a festival. The next day, the people sacrificed burnt offerings and presented fellowship offerings. Then they sat down to eat and drink and got up to indulge in revelry.

God saw this and said to Moses, *"...Go down because your people whom you brought out of Egypt have become corrupt. They have been quick to turn away from what I commanded them..."* (Exodus 32:7.) God then described to Moses exactly what the people had done and said to Moses, *"...they are a stiff-necked people...leave me alone so that my anger may burn against them and that I may destroy them. Then I will make you into a great nation."* (Exodus 32:9-10.)

Moses pleaded with God to relent from destroying the people, and God relented from that action. Nevertheless, there were severe consequences. Moses returned to the camp and saw the golden calf idol and the people running wild. He confronted Aaron, who in keeping with Adam and Eve's shift-the-blame game, said, *"Do not be angry, my lord...you know how prone these people are to evil."* (Exodus 32:22.)

Moses called out to the camp for whoever is with the Lord to come to him. The tribe known as Levites came forward. Moses told them that God had directed that they take swords and *"...go back and forth through the camp from one end to the other, each killing his brother and friend and neighbor."* (Exodus 32:26-27.) The Levites did as commanded; about three thousand of the people died.

Moses returned to Mount Sinai to seek forgiveness for the peoples' sins. God made it clear that He had remained angry with them, and that, in His time, He would punish them for their sins. The Israelites were struck with a plague because of what they had done with the golden calf.

Moses continued to climb Mount Sinai to receive God's instructions. At one point, he asked God to reveal His glory to him. The Lord allowed Moses a glimpse of His glory and proclaimed,

"...The Lord, The Lord, the compassionate and gracious God, slow to anger, abounding in love and faithfulness, maintaining love to thousands, and forgiving wickedness, rebellion, and sin. Yet he does not leave the guilty unpunished; he punishes the children and their children for the sin of the parents to the third and fourth generation." (Exodus 34:6-7.)

God's actions and His proclamations confirm that, although He is merciful to us, there are limits to His forbearance and severe consequences for our disobedience. The fact that He once erased nearly all of creation in the flood should not be lost on us. The Bible tells us that His attributes are unchanging, so we must continue to live mindful that we are not free to go our way and say or do whatever pleases our fleshly desires without eventually paying a price.

The Next Thousand Years

The Israelites eventually broke camp and moved onward. Their journey and history as chronicled in the Old Testament span another thousand years. The exodus from Egypt is dated at about 1,446 BC. The last book of the Old Testament, Malachi, is dated about 430 BC.

During those centuries, Israel's daily life and worship practices were governed by a set of some six-hundred commands and directives known as *"The Law."* The people were told to not intermingle and intermarry with the pagan cultures around them, nor to adopt those cultures' detestable rituals and practices into their lives. During the times when Israel remained faithful and obedient to God, the nation enjoyed prosperity, peace, and some remarkable military victories over its enemies against impossible odds. The nations around them saw this and realized that the one true God of Israel was superior to the many gods and idols they worshipped.

Unfortunately, the Israelites frequently strayed far away from God for extended periods. When they did so, they suffered severe consequences including devastating military defeats and the entire nation being taken into captivity. This up-and-down cycle continued and persisted throughout those times. The repeated lessons of the consequences for disobedience never seemed to sink in permanently.

Prophets And Prophesies

Seventeen of the thirty-nine books of The Old Testament are known as the Books of The Prophets. Most of them bear the name of the prophet by or about whom the book was written. Prophets were men of pure hearts chosen by God to convey God's words to the Israelites. 2 Peter 1:20-21 in the New Testament best describes them:

"Above all, you must understand that no prophecy of Scripture came about by the prophet's own interpretation of things. For prophecy never had its origin in the human will, but prophets, though human, spoke from God as they were carried along by the Holy Spirit."

Throughout this thousand-year period, prophet after prophet repeatedly admonished the Israelites to turn from their sinful ways back to God and warned of the dire consequences God would bring should they fail to do so. The prophets were often ignored. Nevertheless, God in His mercy gave the Israelites ample warning and opportunity to repent before unleashing His wrath.

Isaiah, one of the most renowned prophets, was called by God to cry out against Israel's severe corruption and disobedience about 700 years after the exodus from Egypt:

"Hear me, you heavens! Listen, earth! For the Lord has spoken: 'I reared children (the Israelites) and brought them up, but they have rebelled against me. The ox knows its master, the donkey its owner's manger, but Israel does not know, my people do not understand. Woe to the sinful nation, a people whose guilt is great, a brood of evildoers, children given to corruption! They have forsaken the Lord; they have spurned the Holy One of Israel and turned their backs on him. ... your hands are full of blood! ... Take your evil deeds out of my sight. Stop doing wrong. ... If you are willing and obedient, you will eat the good things of the land; but if you resist and rebel, you will be devoured by the sword.' For the mouth of the Lord has spoken." (Excerpts from Isaiah 1.)

Many years later the Southern kingdom of Israel where Isaiah lived, known as Judah, was conquered by the Babylonians as God brought judgment upon His disobedient people when they failed to heed the prophet's warnings.

In addition to bringing God's corrective warnings to their contemporary fellow Israelites, the prophets also foretold of future events that were and are of critical importance to us today: (1) the birth of Israel's Messiah, Jesus Christ, and (2) a future time known as the *"Last Days"* (and by other similar names) when Jesus will return to earth and all of mankind will face God's final judgment. The Israelites had been conquered and ruled over by other nations often enough that they longed for the foretold appearance of their Messiah, whom they likely believed would be a military leader who would make them victorious over their foes and oppressors.

The vast and remarkable story of Israel in the Old Testament parallels mankind's path to the present. Mankind has continued to distinguish itself with murder, wars, lies, corruption, and the worship and pursuit of contemporary idols like money, power, fame, sex, exotic cars, and bigger and bigger houses, to the exclusion of God. Not only has God been shut out, He is openly disrespected.

The Old Testament ends with a sad depiction of Israel's continuing disobedience. A time-lapse of some four hundred years then ensues for which we have no Biblical accounts. The Bible then resumes with the first book of the New Testament, Matthew.

The New Testament—Our Great Hope & Our Last Chance

As the New Testament begins, Israel is among the many nations conquered by the Roman Empire. From 27 B.C. to 476 A.D., the Roman Empire ruled most of the civilized world. Its reign encompassed 1.7 million square miles. Rome held a firm grip on its vast conquered territory by military force. The Israelites were a nation distinctly different from the pagan nations brought under Roman domination, with centuries of strongly-imbedded religious structures and practices, including their own laws and courts. Israel was also a large enough nation to present a potential challenge to Rome's authority if Rome's iron hand interfered with Israel's religious practices. An uneasy truce developed allowing Israel some measure of religious freedom, but underneath the surface, Israel hated the Roman yoke and imposition of taxes. Underground cells of Israeli rebels simmered, ready to attempt a (hopeless) rebellion against Rome.

Within Israel, the extensive and perhaps complicated law had grown to govern most of the elements of daily life as well as worship and sacrifice rituals. The arbiters of the law were religious officials including priests, Pharisees, teachers of the law, and elders who dressed in finery and were given deference and honor as celebrities in their communities. Their strict and rigid adherence to the law made them, in their own eyes, superior to the average citizens and closer to God. The religious courts and laws were often harsh. A woman caught in adultery was to be stoned to death. Man-made additions, such as dictating the number of steps one was allowed to take on the Sabbath, had made the law oppressive.

Worship took place at the main temple in Jerusalem, a large ornate physical structure with inner and outer courtyards and rooms, whose configuration had been directed by God centuries prior at the time of the exodus from Egypt. The innermost room where God's presence would appear was accessible only to priests, who were the only ones permitted to enter into God's presence for the high ceremonies and sacrifices the law required. Average citizens were barred from the inner chambers. Worship was also conducted at smaller synagogues in outlying areas.

The Birth of Jesus

Within this geopolitical setting, perhaps the most important event in history occurred: the birth of Jesus Christ, a descendant of Abraham and Israel's King David, and God's only begotten son. The story of the first Christmas is familiar to many. A virgin named Mary was pledged to marry a man named Joseph. Before they came together, Mary was visited by the Holy Spirit of God and conceived a child, who was to be called Jesus. Joseph was also visited by an angel of the Lord and was told that Mary's child was conceived by the Holy Spirit and would save his people from their sin. Rather than divorce Mary, Joseph honored what the angel said and took Mary to be his wife. All this took place to fulfill what the Lord foretold through the prophet Isaiah some 700 years earlier:

"The virgin will conceive and give birth to a son, and they will call him Immanuel (which means 'God with us')." (Isaiah 7:14.) Isaiah also proclaimed:

"For unto us a child is born, unto us, a son is given, and the government will be on his shoulders. And he will be called Wonderful Counselor, Mighty God, Everlasting Father, Prince of Peace. Of the greatness of his government and peace, there will be no end. He will reign on David's throne and over his kingdom, establishing and upholding it with justice and righteousness from that time on and forever. The zeal of the Lord Almighty will accomplish this." (Isaiah 9:6-7.)

The birth of Jesus foretold by the prophets was part of God's preordained plan after the fall of mankind in the Garden of Eden to reconcile His wayward children back to Him. In fact, as the One who knows and controls the future, we see this revelation about Jesus in 1 Peter 8:19-20: *"Christ, a lamb without blemish or defect. … was chosen before the creation of the world."* God knew that His lost people could not overcome their sin-natures to live in obedience. The apostle Paul sums up God's plan in Ephesians 1:10: *"…to bring unity to all things in heaven and on earth under Christ."*

Who Was Jesus?

John 3:16 explains who Jesus was (and is), and why God sent Him to us: *"For God so loved the world that he gave his one and only Son, that whoever believes in him shall not perish but have eternal life."*

During His ministry, Jesus was sometimes confronted by Jews who were hostile to Him and His message. Speaking to a group of such angry, disbelieving Jews who challenged His revelation of Himself as the promised Messiah, and who wanted to stone Him for what they considered blasphemy, Jesus said:

"The Father and I are one. ... At my Father's direction, I have done many good works. ... Don't believe me unless I carry out my Father's work. But if I do his work, believe in the evidence of the miraculous works I have done, even if you don't believe me. Then you will know and understand that the Father is in me, and I am in the Father." (John 10:30, 32, 37-38, NLT.)

Here is a mystery we cannot grasp. Jesus was fully God and human at the same time. God manifests Himself in three Persons, known as the Trinity: God the Father, God the Son, and God the Holy Spirit. Yet, He is One God. As we consider God's attributes listed by Tozer, we can see that He has the power to manifest Himself in any form He chooses.

A weak human analogy might be this: water can exist in three forms: (1) ice, a solid; (2) melted ice, a liquid; or (3) boiled away, a vapor that disappears.

Jesus' Life And Ministry

We have little information regarding Jesus' earlier years before He began His three-year earthly ministry at about the age of thirty by being baptized by John the Baptizer.

"As soon as Jesus was baptized, he went up out of the water. At that moment heaven was opened, and he saw the Spirit of God descending like a dove and alighting on him. And a voice from Heaven said, 'This is my Son, whom I love; with him, I am well pleased.'" (Matthew 3:16-17.) There is no mistaking who Jesus is; God Himself proclaimed it.

Jesus gathered together twelve disciples to be His closest companions and began traveling and teaching with them throughout His neighboring regions, proclaiming the radical new covenant between mankind and God, based on salvation achieved by faith and belief in Him rather than by adhering to the law. He instructed people in godly living, performing many miracles to attest to His divinity. He healed the sick, lame and blind, cured lepers, and even raised a man named Lazarus from the dead.

He taught people to love one another, to seek righteousness, to replace pride with humbleness, and to forgive one's enemies rather than seek revenge. He interacted with people shunned by others: tax collectors, prostitutes, lepers, and lower-class citizens, raising the indignation of the Jewish religious leaders—to whom he replied: *"It is not the healthy who need a doctor, but the sick…I have not come to call the righteous, but sinners."* (Matthew 9:12-13.) But perhaps His most striking proclamation was John 14:6: *"I am the way, the truth, and the life. No one comes to the Father except through me."*

God's new covenant entirely replaced the centuries-old law. Jesus' proclamation makes it clear that there is only one way to heaven: through Him. All roads (religions) do **not** lead to the top of the mountain, as quipped by some who think that all religions will eventually get you there. Like so many of our conclusions as to what is true, that one is the polar opposite of reality. Witness Jesus' own words in Matthew 8:13-14:

"Enter through the narrow gate. For wide is the gate and broad is the road that leads to destruction, and many enter through it. But small is the gate and narrow the road that leads to life, and only a few find it."

This particular statement declaring there is but one way to salvation seems to have raised the ire of many in today's world, who think Christians are snobbish and exclusive to claim this, thus confusing the messengers with the message. It is only exclusive in the sense that God has ordained it to be the only way to heaven. But the invitation is not only open to everyone, it is God's desire for everyone to come to Him. Does not the God who created the universe, and us, have the right to determine how we may reconcile our relationship to Him?

"…he (God) is patient with you, not wanting anyone to perish, but everyone to come to repentance." (2 Peter 3:9.)

"For God so loved the world that he gave his one and only son, that whoever believes in him shall not perish but have eternal life. For God did not send his Son into the world to condemn the world, but to save the world through him." (John 3:16-17.)

The Jewish priests and religious leaders were enraged by Jesus' messages and alarmed at the growing number of his followers. If this were not enough, Jesus publicly shamed the religious leaders for their hard hearts and lack of love and compassion. They were blind as to who He was, and perhaps saw themselves potentially losing their jobs and prestige. They began plotting to kill Him. Eventually, they succeeded in having Him arrested after one of His disciples, Judas, betrayed Him.

Jesus's Death

Jesus was tried and convicted on false charges. After being flogged (whipped) on His back until His flesh was raw, He was forced to carry the crossbar of a heavy wooden cross through the streets and up a hill where He was nailed to a cross through His hands and feet. He was left to hang on the cross until He died a slow and agonizing death. Just before He died, *"Jesus cried out in a loud voice, 'My God, My God, why have you forsaken me?'"* (Matthew 27:46.) At that moment, Jesus took on the entire sin of all mankind, and His intimate connection with God was temporarily broken. As we reflect on this, all of our *"whys"* about our own or others' hardships and sufferings should evaporate, as should any questions about how deeply God loves us and how valuable each of us is to Him. The value of something is measured by what someone is willing to pay for it. Rather than spend eternity without us, God chose to sacrifice His only begotten Son to give us the path to eternal life. Why did this have to happen?

Recall that atonement for sin requires a blood sacrifice. For centuries the Israelites were required by the law to offer blood sacrifices of their best- unblemished lambs on a regular, recurring schedule, to atone for their sins. Yet they continued to fall short when it came to how disobediently they lived. Likewise, all of us have sinned and fall short of the glory of God. In His great mercy, God sent His only Son to us, the only One who has lived, and will ever live, a sinless life, to die for us as the sacrificial Lamb of God. Our human depravity was and is so great that it took the death of God's own Son to cleanse us. The following verses inform us:

Hebrews 10:3-4: *"But those (animal) sacrifices (required under the law) are an annual reminder of sins. It is impossible for the blood of bulls and goats to take away sins."*

Romans 3:20-26: *"...no one will be declared righteous in God's sight by the works of the law; rather, through the law, we become conscious of our sin. The righteousness of God is given through faith in Jesus Christ to all who believe for all have sinned and fall short of the glory of God, and all are justified freely by his grace through the redemption that came by Christ Jesus. God presented Christ as a sacrifice of atonement, through the shedding of his blood—to be received by faith."*

Romans 5:12-18 (NLT*): "When Adam sinned, sin entered the world. Adam's sin brought death, so death spread to everyone, for everyone sinned. Adam's one sin brings condemnation for everyone, but Christ's one act of righteousness brings a right relationship with God and new life for everyone."*

To make it clear that our salvation is dependent exclusively upon God's grace and mercy, and not on anything or any works we could ever do, we read:

"As for you (the believers to whom Paul was writing), you were dead in your transgressions and sins, in which you used to live when you followed the ways of this world and the ruler of the kingdom of the air (Satan), the spirit who is now at work in those who are disobedient. All of us lived among them at one time, gratifying the cravings of our flesh and following its desires and thoughts. But because of his great love for us, God, who is rich in mercy, made us alive with Christ even when we were dead in transgressions— ... For it is by grace you have been saved, through faith—and this is not from yourselves, it is the gift of God—not by works, so that no one can boast." (Ephesians 2:1-9.)

Resurrection And Victory

After his death, Jesus' body was prepared for burial and placed in a tomb. A heavy stone was rolled over its entrance. Three days after His burial, two of his disciples, both of whom were named Mary, went to the tomb. The heavy rock had been rolled away and the tomb was empty. They were met by an angel, who said to them,

"…I know that you are looking for Jesus, who was crucified. He has risen, just as he said. Come and see the place where he lay. Then go quickly and tell his disciples: 'He has risen from the dead and is going ahead of you into Galilee. There you will see him.'" (Matthew 28:5-7.)

Jesus had told His disciples several times during His ministry travels that He would be crucified and raised from the dead after three days. Mark 10:32-34 notes one such instance. On the way to Jerusalem with His disciples,

"…he took the Twelve aside and told them what was going to happen to him. 'We are going up to Jerusalem,' he said, 'and the Son of Man will be delivered over to the chief priests and the teachers of the law. They will condemn him to death and will hand him over to the Gentiles, (Roman authorities) who will mock him and spit on him, flog him and kill him. Three days later he will rise.'" (See also Matthew 17:22-23.)

The two Marys did as they were told and reported to the disciples that Jesus had risen.

Many of the people who encountered Jesus after His resurrection were listed previously. Acts 1:3, written by the apostle Luke, adds:

"After his suffering (death and resurrection) he presented himself to them (the disciples) and gave many convincing proofs that he was alive. He appeared to them over a period of forty days and spoke about the kingdom of God."

Some forty days after His reappearance, Jesus was taken up into the sky as the disciples watched, and is now seated in heaven at God's right hand. Acts 1:10-11:

"They were looking intently up into the sky as he was going when suddenly two men dressed in white (angels) stood beside them. 'Men of Galilee,' they said, 'why do you stand here looking into the sky? This same Jesus, who has been taken from you into heaven will come back in the same way you have seen him go into heaven.'"

Jesus has promised that He will return to earth, at which time He will gather His children. He told His disciples this shortly before His death:

"My Father's house has many rooms; if that were not so, would I have told you that I am going there to prepare a place for you? And if I go to prepare a place for you, I will come back and take you to be with me that you also may be where I am." (John 14:2-3.)

Matthew 24:30-31 (NLT) provide a stunning picture of Jesus' return:

"And then, at last, the sign that the Son of Man is coming will appear in the heavens, and there will be deep mourning among all the peoples of the earth. And they will see the Son of Man coming on the clouds of heaven with power and great glory. And he will send out his angels with the mighty blast of a trumpet and they will gather his chosen ones from all over the world – from the farthest ends of the earth and heaven."

This will occur in conjunction with the end times when God will judge all mankind. We all get one chance, our mortal lifespan, to get it right.

"Just as people are destined to die once, and after that to face judgment, so Christ was sacrificed once to take away the sins of many; and he will appear a second time, not to bear sin, but to bring salvation to those who are waiting for him." (Hebrews 9:27-28.)

Before He departed from earth, Jesus commissioned His disciples to carry the message of the gospel, the new covenant of redemption through His death and resurrection, to the ends of the earth. From this handful of men, His message has spread and thrived for over 2,000 years despite continual efforts to extinguish it. The message was first intended for the Israelites, God's originally-chosen people, who were steeped in the concept of the necessity of a blood sacrifice to atone for sin. They should have understood and accepted the evidence that Jesus was their promised Messiah and how His sacrifice was meant as final and complete payment for their sins. But most Israelites did not receive Him as their own. Moreover, their religious leaders persecuted Him and His followers, both before and after His crucifixion

In His great mercy, God commissioned apostles to spread the gospel to the Gentiles (all peoples other than the Jews) as well, affording salvation to anyone who placed their faith and trust in Jesus and His resurrection.

Aside from a small number, the Jewish people of today largely continue to follow the law rather than Jesus. They do not recognize or acknowledge Him as the promised Messiah. There are Bible passages such as Romans 11:25-36 that speak of a time when those who are Israelites by descent may come to faith in Jesus. They have alternate interpretations requiring reference to other passages and are ancillary to the topic of this treatise.

While this subject sometimes causes friction between Jews and Christians, this should not be so. God loves both groups, and we are commanded to love one another. Salvation through, and only through, Jesus was made known and available to everyone universally, and it remains so today. God's promise to Abraham over two-thousand years before Jesus' birth is fulfilled in Jesus.

Judgement Day

No one knows how long they have to live. Not only can our lives end suddenly and unexpectedly, but the imminent return of Jesus will occur in a fraction of a second at a time known only to God, meaning we had best not put off our decision as to whether or not to accept him as our Lord and Savior. 2 Peter 3:10-12:

"But the day of the Lord will come like a thief. The heavens will disappear with a roar; the elements will be destroyed by fire, and the earth and everything in it will be laid bare. Since everything will be destroyed in this way, what kind of people ought you to be?"

We should consider our inevitable judgment by God with righteous fear. Jesus said this to His disciples in Luke 12:4-5 (NLT):

"Dear friends, don't be afraid of those who want to kill your body; they cannot do any more to you after that. But I'll tell you whom to fear. Fear God, who has the power to kill you and then throw you into hell. Yes, he's the one to fear."

Many passages describe the judgment everyone will face before God. We may think we get away with a lot during our lives, but nothing escapes God's notice. Here is one depiction which ought to capture everyone's attention, Revelation 20:11-15. This is part of the vision the apostle John was given shortly before his death:

"Then I saw a great white throne and him who was seated on it. The earth and the heavens fled from his presence, and there was no place for them. And I saw the dead, great and small, standing before the throne, and books were opened. Another book was opened, which is the book of life. The dead were judged according to what they had done as recorded in the books. The sea gave up the dead that were in it, and death and Hades gave up the dead that were in them, and each person was judged according to what they had done. Then death and Hades were thrown into the lake of fire. The lake

of fire is the second death. Anyone whose name was not found written in the book of life was thrown into the lake of fire."

The book of life contains the names of all those who have chosen to accept Jesus as their Lord and Savior and the salvation that comes from Jesus' death on the cross and His resurrection. He paid for their sins, just as He paid for mine and yours so that no one who believes in him would face God's judgment for their sins: *"...everyone who believes in him receives forgiveness of sins through his name."* (Acts 10:43.) And as Paul and Barnabas preached after Jesus' death:

"Therefore, my friends, I want you to know that through Jesus, the forgiveness of sins is proclaimed to you. Through him, everyone who believes is set free from every sin, a justification you were not able to obtain under the law of Moses."

How Long Is Forever?

Genesis revealed that mankind was originally destined to live forever in fellowship with our eternal God. That intent was temporarily derailed when sin and death entered the world. But the Bible makes it clear that God's eternal kingdom will be restored in conjunction with the last days. The Old Testament prophets first proclaimed this.

Isaiah 45:17: *"But Israel will be saved by the Lord with everlasting salvation;…"*

Isaiah 51:6: *"…the heavens will vanish like smoke, the earth will wear out like a garment and its inhabitants die like flies. But my salvation will last forever,…"*

Daniel 2:44: *"…the God of heaven will set up a kingdom that will never be destroyed…it will itself endure forever."*

Isaiah 12:1-2: *"…There will be a time of distress such as has not happened from the beginnings of nations until then. But at that time your people—everyone whose name is found written in the book—will be delivered. Multitudes who sleep in the dust of the earth will awake: some to everlasting life, others to shame and everlasting contempt."*

The New Testament apostles confirm these prophecies.

1 Thessalonians 4:16-17: *"For the Lord himself will come down from heaven with a loud command, with the voice of the archangel and with the trumpet call of God, and the dead in Christ will rise first. After that, we who are still alive and are left will be caught up together with them in the clouds to meet the Lord in the air. And we will be with the Lord forever."*

1 John 2:12: *"The world and its desires pass away, but whoever does the will of God lives forever."*

Eternity in the lake of fire (hell) is one of the two possible destinies we all face after our physical death. Eternity in heaven is the other one.

Remember God's stated desire is that no one should perish. We have a choice of destination. He awaits our decision.

"Here I am! I stand at the door and knock. If anyone hears my voice and opens the door, I will come in and eat with that person, and they with me." (Revelation 3:20.)

Jesus stands at the door of your life, awaiting only your decision to let Him in.

The Bible gives us some indications of what heaven and hell are like. The depictions of God's wrath and the torment of hell are frightening. In 2 Peter 2:4-5 we see these:

"God did not spare the angels when they sinned, but sent them to hell, putting them in chains of darkness to be held for judgment; …he did not spare the ancient world when he brought the flood on its ungodly people,…"

Matthew 8:12 notes that those who reject faith in Jesus, *"…will be thrown outside, into the darkness, where there will be weeping and gnashing of teeth."* And in Revelation 20:10 we see a fate reserved for Satan and his end-time companions, the beast, and the false prophet: *"…thrown into the lake of burning sulfur,…they will be tormented day and night for ever and ever."*

One of the better depictions of heaven is found in these excerpts from Revelation 21:3-27:

"… Look! God's dwelling place is now among the people, and he will dwell with them. They will be his people, and God himself will be with them and be their God. He will wipe every tear from their eyes. There will be no more death or mourning or crying or pain, for the old order of things has passed away…. It (heaven) shone with the glory of God, and its brilliance was like that of a very precious jewel, like a jasper, clear as crystal. … The wall was made of jasper, and the city of pure gold, as pure as glass. The foundations of the city walls were decorated with every kind of precious stone … jasper, … sapphire, … agate, … emerald, … onyx, … ruby, … chrysolite, … beryl, … topaz, … turquoise, … jacinth, … amethyst. The twelve gates were twelve pearls,

each gate made of a single pearl. The great street of the city was gold, as pure as transparent glass. ... Nothing impure will ever enter it, nor will anyone who does what is shameful or deceitful, but only those whose names are written in the book of life."

Revelation 22:1-5 continue the vision given to the apostle John: . . . *"Then the angel showed me the river of the water of life, as clear as crystal, flowing from the throne of God and of the Lamb (Jesus) down the middle of the great street of the city. On each side of the river stood the tree of life, bearing twelve crops of fruit, yielding its fruit every month. And the leaves of the tree are for the healing of the nations. They will not need the light of a lamp or the light of the sun, for the Lord God will give them light. And they will reign forever and ever."*

We are also told that those who will pass on to heaven will do so with entirely new bodies, spiritual in nature. Excerpts from 1 Corinthians 15:35-58 tell us this: *"...flesh and blood cannot inherit the kingdom of God, nor does the perishable inherit the imperishable. ... We will not all sleep, but we will all be changed—in a flash, in the twinkling of an eye, at the last trumpet."* (see 1 Thessalonians 4:13-17 and the trumpet judgments referenced in Revelation). *"For the trumpet will sound, the dead will be raised imperishable, and we will be changed. For the perishable must clothe itself with the imperishable, and the mortal with immortality, then the saying that is written, (the Old Testament prophecies from Isaiah 25:8 and Hosea 13:14), will come true: 'Death has been swallowed up in victory.' 'Where, O death, is your victory? Where, O death, is your sting?'"*

The Redeemed Life

Eternal life in Heaven is but one of the blessings we receive when we accept Jesus as our Lord and Savior. There is much more for us during our lifetimes, so much that only a thorough study of the Bible can reveal it all. God has created each of us for a purpose. He equips believers with spiritual gifts to accomplish those purposes. We are new creations in Him, and no longer need to be controlled by our fleshly desires—unless we choose to give in to them.

Everyone who surrenders their life to Jesus will be blessed with the Holy Spirit, to guide them into the truth and enable them to overcome the temptations to indulge in the lifestyles prompted by our selfish urges and desires. A life lived in tune with the Spirit is full *of "…love, joy, peace, forbearance, kindness, goodness, faithfulness, gentleness, and self-control."* (Galatians 5:22-23.) This is the life we strive for out of gratitude and obedience to our Lord and Savior. And doesn't this life seem more attractive than one filled with turmoil, anxiety, fear, and endless striving for all the shiny material objects we chase after? Isn't this a better foundation upon which to endure the social and worldwide disintegration that surrounds us today? In contrast to life in the Spirit,

"The acts of the flesh are obvious: sexual immorality, impurity, and debauchery, idolatry, and witchcraft; hatred, discord, jealousy, fits of rage, selfish ambition, dissensions, factions, and envy; drunkenness, orgies, and the like." (Galatians 5:19-21.)

The differences between worldly life and a Godly life are stark. We are constantly challenged by the allure of worldly pursuits and pleasures. Even after accepting Jesus as our Lord and Savior, we will occasionally fail, for we remain flawed people. Our sinful natures remain inside us, in conflict with our desires to live as changed people.

Are We Almost Out Of Time?

In addition to the events that more commonly bring about the end of our lives such as accidents, illness, and old age, there is the wild card that may show up at any time that will affect the entire planet. Extended discussions of the end times, or the last days, have filled many books over the years, without consistent agreement among even theologians as to how these times will unfold. I include mention of this topic because it is of significant importance and because there is currently a widespread feeling that these times are imminent.

The last days, or end times, will coincide with the return of Jesus to earth, combined with a time of, according to most prevailing views, cataclysmic judgments rained upon the Earth by God as described in Revelation. An analysis of what to expect must include a synthesis of the prophecies by Old Testament prophets, signs of the approach of those times given by Jesus to His disciples, and an analysis of the difficult-to-interpret book of Revelation. The challenge becomes understanding how all of these pieces work together to form a picture, much like trying to complete a jigsaw puzzle that is missing key pieces. We are given as much information as God intended for us to have, which still leaves some unanswered questions. A complication arises in that some of the descriptions of the tribulations point to events already past, such as the destruction of the Jewish Temple and Jerusalem in 70 A.D. by the Romans, as well as similar events foreshadowed to be repeated in our future.

There are some aspects beyond debate, simply because the Bible makes them plain: (1) Jesus will return to earth to gather his children; (2) no one knows the day or hour when this will occur except the Lord God Himself; (3) Jesus' return will happen suddenly, in a fraction of a second; (4) all of mankind, living and dead, will face judgment at God's hand; (5) only those whose names are written in the book of life will pass on to Heaven. Left for spirited debate are the questions of whether or not believers will escape from, or suffer through, the end time tribulations, and how to interpret the tribulations—as literal, figurative, or both; and as past, present, future, or some combination.

Several signs have been given to us that signal the approach of those times. I only mention some of them to provide a sample of the evidence cited by those who think we are near, or on the verge of, Jesus' return. To maintain perspective, in 1970, a Dallas Theological Seminary graduate, author, and evangelist Hal Lindsey published a popular book entitled *The Late, Great, Planet Earth,* suggesting that the world was on the verge of the end times. The Middle East was embroiled in a level of turmoil at that time sufficient to suggest that possibility, having witnessed Israel's victory in the 1967 *"Six-Day War"* between Israel and Arab factions in which Jerusalem was reunified under Israeli rule. Yet here we are, a half-century later, admittedly in worse chaos, but still mostly intact.

Matthew 24 contains Jesus' answer to his apostles' questions of what would be the signs of the end times. It should be read in its entirety; only a portion is quoted here:

"...Watch out that no one deceives you. For many will come in my name claiming, "I am the Messiah," and will deceive many. You will hear of wars and rumors of wars but see to it that you are not alarmed. Such things must happen, but the end is still to come. Nation will rise against nation and kingdom against kingdom. There will be famines and earthquakes in various places. All these are the beginning of birth pains. Then you will be handed over to be persecuted and put to death, and you will be hated by all nations because of me. At that time many will turn away from the faith and will betray and hate each other, and many false prophets will appear and deceive many people. Because of the increase of wickedness, the love of most will grow cold, but the one who **stands firm** *to the end will be saved (emphasis supplied). And this gospel of the kingdom will be preached in the whole world as a testimony to all nations, and then the end will come."*

The exhortation to stand firm to the end is emphasized because it is repeated over and over throughout the New Testament due to its critical importance. We are going to face exceptional difficulties towards and during the end times, but those who stand firm and do not lose faith will reach their reward. The need to stand firm in faith no matter what we face is a more important concept to be grasped from the end-times discussions than what will happen or how those times might unfold.

As our social and political fabric disintegrates around us, many are citing this passage as another sign that the end times are approaching, 2 Timothy 3:1-5:

"But mark this: There will be terrible times in the last days. People will be lovers of themselves, lovers of money, boastful, proud, abusive, disobedient to their parents, ungrateful, unholy, without love, unforgiving, slanderous, without self-control, brutal, not lovers of good, treacherous, rash, conceited, lovers of pleasure rather than lovers of God—having a form of godliness but denying its power. ..."

This certainly describes our present times, sadly including many of our elected officials.

While there is much more to the question, such as the formation of Israel as a nation with geographic boundaries in 1948, that would support a conclusion that we are almost there, the bottom line seems to be: we don't know, but each day we draw closer and we need to be ready. All of the events and behaviors outlined in Matthew 24 and 2 Timothy can certainly characterize our present days, but they can also be applied to past, or even future, times as well. Just as our deaths will terminate our opportunity to choose, the sudden return of Jesus will terminate that opportunity for all of mankind.

It's Now Up To You

If at any time you choose to accept Jesus as your Lord and Savior, a simple prayer like this, coming from your heart, is all that is needed:

Lord Jesus, I want you to come into my life. Thank you for dying on the cross for my sins. I receive you as my Lord and Savior. Thank you for forgiving my sins and giving me eternal life. Please make me the kind of person you want me to be. In Jesus' name, Amen.

If you are considering this but are hesitant to take the step, you might want to ask yourself what's stopping you, and what is gained (or what might be lost) by delay. Trying to remain neutral is the same as rejecting Jesus. In His own words, *"Anyone who isn't with me opposes me, and anyone who isn't working with me is actually working against me."* (Matthew 12:30, NLT.)

Choosing to follow Jesus is just the beginning of your journey. If you do not own a Bible, acquire one. A study Bible with marginal notes that explain difficult passages is helpful. Websites like everystudent.com help answer many of the questions you will have. It is important to connect with a Bible-based church and other believers for fellowship, support, and learning. Faith needs to grow and strengthen, and without their support, it is all too easy for faith to falter when life's difficulties show up, and show up they will. We are told that we will all face trials and tribulations. Facing them alone can be devastating. But we have the promise that those who persevere in faith to the end will receive their place in heaven.

If you are still uncertain about all of this, consider asking God in prayer to show you the truth. He will answer those who earnestly seek Him. Proverbs 8:17:

"I love those who love me, and those who seek me find me."

About The Author

James Downey holds a B.S. in Psychology and a Juris Doctor degree in Law from the University of Nebraska. After serving a term in the U.S. Army, he practiced law in Colorado for 30 years, retiring in 2004. In the 1980s he began an ongoing comparative religion study, exploring Buddhism, Hinduism, Taoism, New Age, Catholicism, Islam, Jehovah's Witnesses, Mormonism, Judaism, and the primary Protestant denominations. He has attended and taught in denominational and community churches in four different states. Travels to Fiji, Eastern Europe, Russia, Turkey, Israel, Jordan, Egypt, and The Vatican added first-hand exposure to the variety of beliefs and practices among different faiths

Dying to Live is his fourth book. His first book, *The Evolution of Jihad*, written under the pen name of H. Davidson, explores the roots of Islam and how the search for the One True God of Abraham led to the terrorism we face today. His second book, *Why?*, posits an answer to the question of why the world is so full of chaos and misery if there is a God who loves us. In a shift of direction, his third book, *Brothers in Arms*, recounts memoirs and life stories of veterans, victims, heroes, and survivors of WWII, the Korean War, and the Vietnam War. Their stories are accompanied by 130 historic documents and photographs, many from their own personal collections. All of his books are available at amazon.com. (Several books entitled *Brothers in Arms* are in print. The author's Amazon and book link is:

amazon.com/gp/product/B0846459NY).

The author can be contacted at j.d.vrod@gmail.com.

Bibliography And Other Resources

The Knowledge of the Holy, by A.W. Tozer, © 1961 by Aiden W. Tozer, HarperCollins Publishers, 195 Broadway, New York, NY 10007.

The Case for Faith, by Lee Strobel, © 2000 by Lee Strobel, Zondervan, Grand Rapids, MI 49520.

Universe—The Definitive Visual Guide, © 2005, 2008, Dorling Kindersley Limited, DK Publishing, 375 Hudson St., New York, New York 10014.

Alert! Perilous Times, by James A. Durham, © 2018, James A. Durham, DESTINY IMAGE ® PUBLISHERS, INC., P.O. Box 310, Shippensburg, PA 17257-0310.

The Grand Canyon, Evolution, and Intelligent Design, by Dr. Richard S. Beal, Jr., © 2007, Richard S. Beal, Jr., Lighthouse Christian Publishing, 5531 Dufferin Drive, Savage, MN 55378.

EveryStudent.com ®

Creation.com (Creation Ministries)

Unless otherwise indicated, Scripture texts and some references to marginal comments used in this work are derived from The NIV Quest Study Bible published by Zondervan, Grand Rapids, MI 49546, © 1994, 2003, 2011 by Zondervan; NEW INTERNATIONAL VERSION ®. NIV ® are registered trademarks of Biblica, Inc. ®. Used by permission of Zondervan. All rights reserved worldwide.

Scripture quotations marked NLT are derived from the Holy Bible, New Living Translation, Copyright © 1996, 2004, 2015 by Tyndale House

Made in the USA
Middletown, DE
28 March 2022

63250463R00054